I'm so proud of you Grandma

I am so proud to have such a wonderful Grandma.

You are caring.

You are kind.

You have loved me since before I was even born.

I am so proud of the way you keep going.

Even on hard days, you get up,
and get on with whatever needs doing.

That takes strength.

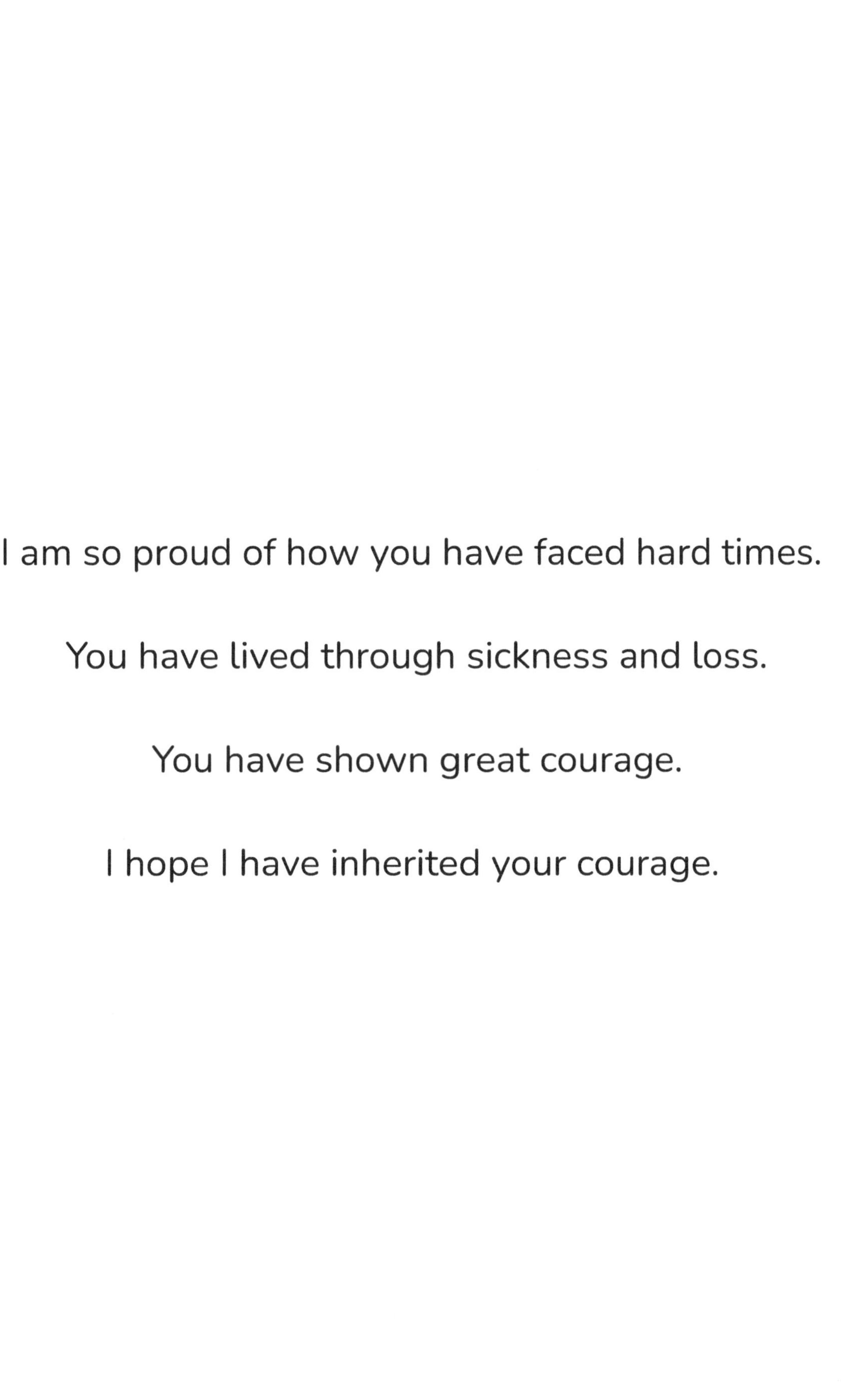

I am so proud of how you have faced hard times.

You have lived through sickness and loss.

You have shown great courage.

I hope I have inherited your courage.

I am so proud of how you have handled change.

A new home.

New routines.

New people.

That is a lot to cope with - and you do so with a brave face.

I am proud of the way you are letting others
help you.

You have always been the one to help
everyone else.

But now it is your turn to receive.

You are doing so well.

Looking back, I am so proud of your work and
your career.

You gave your best every day - sometimes in
difficult circumstances.

You made a difference in many people's lives.

I hope I am following in your footsteps.

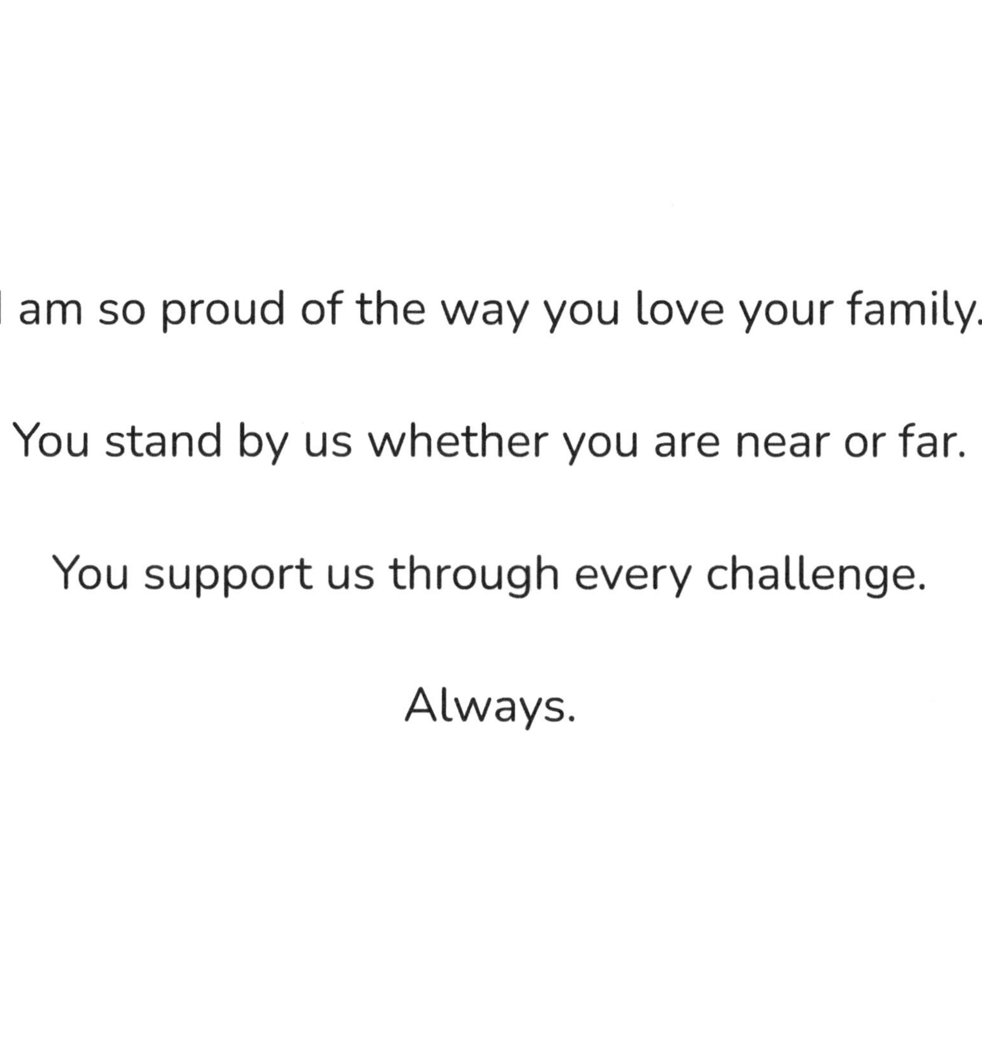

I am so proud of the way you love your family.

You stand by us whether you are near or far.

You support us through every challenge.

Always.

I am so proud of the way your home feels like
my home too.

A home full of warmth.

Laughter.

And love for all the people and
pets who passed through.

I am so proud of your friendships.

You care so deeply about your friends.

And they care about you.

I am blessed to have learnt about the
importance of friendship from you.

I am so proud of the way you smile when
you see me walk through the door.

I know you see my big smile shining right
back at you.

I love the way we can read or play together,
passing the time without a care in the
world.

I am so proud of how you care for your
children and your granchildren.

You are patient.

You are gentle.

You show them love every day.

I am so proud of your wisdom.

You have taught me so much - about love,
about commitment, about how to be the
best person I can be.

I am still learning from you.

I am so proud of your compassion.

You see the good in people.

You care.

You show great patience and strength
when helping those in need.

You always have.

I am so proud of your loyalty.

To your family.

To your friends.

To the things you believe in.

I am so proud that you keep learning.

You stay curious.

You keep trying new things.

You have taught me what matters most.

Love.

Strength.

Kindness.

Family.

Friendship.

All of this is to say -
I am so proud of you, Grandma!

And because I am like you in many ways...
I am proud of me too.